YOUR BODY SHOULD BE
A PART OF THE WORLD

ELLEN SAMUELS

C&R Press
Conscious & Responsible

Cover art by Sally Bachner
Cover design by Rebecca Targ

C&R Press
Conscious & Responsible
crpress.org

For discounted purchases, please contact: C&R Press sales@crpress.org

YOUR BODY SHOULD BE A PART OF THE WORLD

For my disabled kin,
my sick loves,
my lovely cripples,
every one who belongs to this world

TABLE OF CONTENTS

i.

On the Hospital   14
Yesterday I Apologized   16
After the Procedure   18
Sick and Well Time   20

ii.

Plum Tomato   24
Melon   25
Dragon's Tongue Bean   26
Tomatillos   27
Bitternut Hickory   28
Sweet Basil   30
Eggplant/Aubergine   32

iii.

Cigarette-Paper Scars   35
My Mother Always Had Numbers   37
Pericardial Effusion   39
Pruning the Yew   40

iv.

In Answer to Your Question   43
Elegy for a Mask Mandate   45
To the Doctor Who Said I Am Not One of The   47

Acknowledgements   50
Notes   51
About the Author   53

i.

On The Hospital

When I say I'm at the hospital, everyone sits up and pays atten-
tion. The hospital is serious. The hospital means business. *Is there
anything we can do?* people say to the hospital.

But the hospital is just a place I go sometimes when I'm well
enough to leave my house.

All these weeks and months I spend at home, drifting the plumb
of bed's expanse. The hospital is not a building. The hospital is
here, this pale inland sea.

My mouth is the hospital, opening for the words I can't think
how to say.

My hands are the hospital, reaching for the spoon handle before
it drops.

The sound of the spoon hitting the floor is the hospital.

The hospital is the shirt I unpeel from my heat-slick back, and
the clean shirt I take from the stack and drag over my head is the
hospital.

The basket of unfolded laundry in the living room all week is the
hospital.

In the center of my heartbone I feel the hospital beating, through
days and nights that bleed into days as a pink-coated pill touched
with wet fingers leaks its shell until you decide whether to take it
or throw it away.

My dog's grunts and startles beside me, her trembling repetitive
dreams, are the hospital.

The sour at the back of my throat when my breath stops in the
folds of night tastes of the hospital.

The pillow I twist to an easier spot, the sheet that escapes the mattress corner, the quilt knotted around my belly, these are the hospital.

This animal burrow, this rumpled cot, fevered skin and dog's fur and cotton sheets all petaled together, this is the hospital. And it is home. This is home and the hospital.

Yesterday, I Apologized

Yesterday, I apologized to the dog
for not being able to walk her,

anymore, to the moss-green lake
in the dappled light, her nose

tender against my palm, sampling
fish-reek and the wind's news.

Yesterday, I apologized to the middle
of my middle finger, the years-old

pebble under skin, bone-knot
bunched in memory's string. I said

I'm sorry to the skin's warp
and weft, to the nerve strung

tight on the knuckle's fret. I said I'm
sorry to the skin itself, curtain

roughly drawn across the body's
pink. I apologized to sacrum

and thighbone, to the hinge
unhinging where it used to

swing, striding next to the dog
on our afternoon walks.

Yesterday, I apologized
to the nightstand where bottles

jostle and crowd with
last year's books. I sent

my regrets to the rutted bed
where I knelt each summer

pulling sorrel and dandelion, snow-
on-the-mountain and creeping

Charlie, in the ripe dirt-
smell and welter of heat.

Last night, when I lay down
on the smooth relief of pillow

and sheet, I closed my eyes
and apologized to the insides

of my eyelids, as if two moths
having settled there, needed to know

what would happen next. Close
your wings, I said, stay with

me in the moon-wet night. We
have done all we can.

After the Procedure

I didn't know I could
be broken in places
that were already

broken, blood-
tunnels weaving through
old bruise. When

that doctor put his
hands on me, he was not
prepared, I was

not prepared
for how loud my voice
could sound. And the

wrack of bone
against bone. The syringe-
screw. The counting. All

these alphabets
I didn't know
could be un-learned

and written again, in
an afternoon. And
could I be the same

person today,
harvesting mint's bitter
with bare

hands, chewing
wood sorrel's lemon-
sweet buds? I don't

know how
to know myself
anymore, how

even to see
my own skin's
ground. I forgot

to look in the mirror
for days. Still
in the garden, I find

myself, untangling
devil's thorn from
among the lilacs, handling

each needled stem
back to the root. And
the angled knife,

the shovel, boiling
water from the stove. This
is how you bury it

so it doesn't come
back. All
afternoon, this long,

tired work, the sun
an eye overhead, a lens,
white-hot.

Sick and Well Time

I have to write down somewhere how I feel on the days when I don't move and I don't stay still. When my legs slide over the bed-edge and I'm walking to the bathroom, putting toothpaste on the brush, tasting mint on my tongue—and still part of me is back in the bed, folding and unfolding the edge of the sheet like a bit of finger-skin almost scraped off.

My left vertebral artery has separated just a bit, dissected they call it, its inside wall shredded like a green twig trying not to bend. So now I live in a world of spinning, some days just a faint humming inside my skull, others a swooping roller coaster through a too-bright, too-loud tunnel of nerves.

On a good day, you wouldn't know to look at me there was anything wrong. On a good day, all anyone sees is the cherry pop lipstick from Lord and Taylor and the twelve silver ring-splints on my fingers and the thick long hair that gets curlier as I grow older, that stays brown and refuses to gray.

On a good day, am I sick or am I well?

If I feel strong, if I heft the groceries into the car and chop the carrots for soup and write these words, if I sing to my dog as she follows me through the house grinning and shaking her ears... How can I be sick, on a good day?

And if I can't figure it out myself, how can I expect anyone else to understand?

*

On a bad day, I don't remember what it's like to be well. The sick world is the solid world, the real one.

Maybe you know this world as well. It's the world where you struggle to sit up to drink without spilling. Where you spill anyway, cool

Your Body Should Be A Part of the World

liquid dribbling down your chin, dampness soaking through your thin pajama top.

It's the damp faint stickiness of skin, and the faint damp stickiness of sheets, and you between them nothing but breath, in and out, trying to hold on.

*

Today started as a bad day, but in the afternoon my head felt clearer so I stepped outside to let the dog chase squirrels while I walked the twelve feet to the vegetable garden.

As always, there was so much needing to be done, wild sorrel and purslane breaking through the mulch, tomato and pepper plants drooping into heavy tangles. My pajama strap snagged on a branch as I inched between the tallest tomatoes, snapping off a few of their blighty stems.

But as I edged further, I saw the plants were already covered in blight, its leopard-yellow spots swarming the drooped leaves.

Every year I promise myself to keep up with the pruning, and every year I spend more days in bed and fewer in the garden.

Today it seemed more impossible than ever. My hands were already trembling. When I crouched to reach the lowest stems, I lost my balance and flailed for something to hold. The flimsy tomato cage sank to its knees as I fell heavily sideways.

My pajama legs were stained brown with cocoa mulch and pollen. I smelled the sharp tang of tomato leaves all around me.

And then, hidden behind leaves so I almost missed them, on the lowest stem of the Early Girl plant, I saw three small green tomatoes, the first of the season. Smooth-skinned, hard as stones, the size of my knuckles. The leaves were blighted but the fruit was clean.

*

Are the tomatoes sick or well? The only answer is that they are both. And like them, I have to find a way to live in both worlds. It will never be easy.

I want to curl up like the blighted leaves I've pruned away, sink back into the soil, be done with moving.

But somehow I wake up again every morning, still spinning, still unfolding, a green stone packed tight with seeds, holding hard to the dirt-sweet heart of this world.

ii.

Plum Tomato
Solanum lycopersicum

Your body should be mute
as this globed fruit
in a hollow of leaves
heavy and red.

What you wish
sometimes
when the night draws deep
is for someone else
to be able to hear you.

What you wish sometimes
is for anyone else
to lay a hand
across your back and feel
its thrumming.

It is either pain
or the absence of pain
that defines you. You forget
sometimes how to
tell the difference
between stem and root.

Your body should be
a part of the world, or the
world should be a part
of your body. You forget

sometimes how to tell
the difference
between pulp and skin.
Both over so soon,
so sweet.

Melon
Cucumis melo

A scoop out
of the middle of you.
Sugar in the palm.

The garden is never
long enough
for the vine. You cast

through soil
for a place to sink.
Seeds nestle

in the heart-
hollow, waiting
to be used up

and the body
softens until even
your shell forgets

its shape.

Dragon's Tongue Bean
Phaseolus vulgaris

I am only beautiful
if left alone: language
a purple blur

against skin. Here
find my ribs, ordered
and particular; here

find my heart,
memory's fiddle
stone, spring-

split egg. O
leave me alone with
my crisp bones, let

me tell you later
of winter.

Tomatillo
Physalis ixocarpa

The husk forms
first. Yellow
flower into globe

paper lantern
lime-fist
so empty your

finger dents
its cheek. Slowly
rain dirt gather

into compact
moon, ripened
stone. Is this

how the body
outlives its
shell? No soul

rising to heaven,
just the skin's
slow upheaval

into green.

Bitternut Hickory
Carya Cordiformis

for B.F.

There's a
poem I promised
myself to write,

once I'd peeled
every ocher
purse into ragged

moon, once
I'd wheedled the
catkins out

of my hair, once
I'd numbered
the pinnates on

every leaf. But
already the bodies
are settling

into August
ground where no
one will sniff,

gnaw, swallow,
digest them: no one
will hunger

them back to
the earth. Still they
will furrow, take

root, and rot their
way to eternal
life. And if I had

written this poem
for you, like I
promised, that is

what it would say.

Sweet Basil
Ocimum basilicum

I never thought
I'd have my mother's
hands that knew

how to dead-
head blooms to draw
new growth. I never

guessed I would find
myself, two years
older than her

second cancer, four
years younger
than she was at

death, kneeling
in the ripe fathom
of earth, feeling

with her familiar
hands along
the stem of the

great-leafed herb
to the joint's
thick, digging my

nail to loosen
its double heart.
In the basket

I pile these small
lessons, jade
creased into old

silk, sharp
scent of what's
left behind.

Eggplant/Aubergine
solanum melongena

It's because I don't
want to be my mother
that I am finally

letting her go. It's
because the eggplant
grows so heavy

I have to twine
its stem against this
stake. It's because

the time to maturity
is longer in a wintered
climate I have to

buy my seedlings
from another house.
It's because purple-

black absorbs
the sun's travel it
grows so fast. It's

because the electric
scalpel can both un-
close and seal the

wound, the surgeon
can lift all my
roundness out

where everyone can
see how much I
don't want to be

my mother, how
thick the flesh is
under the knife,

how hard it tries
not to be cut.

iii.

Cigarette-Paper Scars

My mother's scars were wide gashes of white across chest and belly, cut across with lines where the stitches had been, like railroad tracks, like a line of lower case "t"s, like mouths trapped in the middle of speaking and filled with flour smoothed flat by a knife.

In fourth grade, I opened a book about Norway and saw a map of my mother's scars. A jagged finger stretched from sea into land, across the right side of her torso, away from the soft droop of her breast.

She tucked her prosthesis in its private pocket as I watched her getting ready for work. Dense beige jelly, heavy in my hand while she drew on her lipstick, standing in her slip in front of the mirror.

It took longer to recover from her second surgery. Maybe the radiation, she said. This scar cut straight down the middle of her, an open zipper riding her swell. The staples left lines, moth's-wing white, thick punctuation marks riding the vertical incision.

The scar on her chest flattened her, left her lopsided and hollow. But the scar on her belly split her open, never quite losing its angry red edge, the hint of what was taken: the ovary with its bulbous tumor, the tubes, the uterus a red purse shrunken by chemo that saved her life nine years before. It was worth giving it all up, she told me more than once.

The first time I saw a picture of a mastectomy scar, Matuschka on the cover of *New York Times* magazine the year after my mother died, I was surprised by its narrow, almost elegant lines, like lips drawn thin with disapproval.

I thought my mother's scar must be different because she had her operation in a more brutal time. I knew doctors used to cut out even more, taking the entire chest muscle, leaving women unable to lift their arms overhead. I supposed techniques had evolved, surgeons had learned to knit the skin back together more tightly. I had no reason to think any differently.

But then the doctors began to turn my skin inside-out, to read it like a diary I didn't remember keeping. Then I learned how my mother's body lived inside mine, a jangling skeleton held together with loose pins, our DNA a sea of dropped stitches.

So the same thin knife that slipped cleanly through other women's skin opened an ivory canyon on my mother, thick rush of white rising to fill that spreading sea, the one I saw in the mirror, the one neither of us knew was never supposed to stretch so wide.

My Mother Always Had Numbers

My mother always had numbers
on her mind, and one of those
was the number of times

she closed her office door so
no one could ask her
for tea or directions. Each

morning she solved
the equation *woman*: Cut most
of your hair. Long

earrings signal desire. Pure
and thirstless, don't
wear high heels. She sketched

theorems on napkins,
served them up
with the breakfast eggs.

When the promotion
finally arrived, they told her
to write the job

description. It read: *A woman,*
dying in her forties. It
read: Your daughter

will never study
calculus. It read: The tumor
came back too

soon. My mother
always had numbers on her
mind, and one of those

was the day I was
born. And one of those
was a closed door. And

the rest were all zero,
zero, the world remade
by the discovery of zero.

Pericardial Effusion

Did you know the heart
floats in its own sea, never
fully still? Did you feel
the waves overtaking the
shores, your heart a
wild buoy in their grasp? If
you're surprised, you've never
paid attention to the
tides. Anyone who's heard
about that ten-year-old
girl driven out from Ohio
to deliver her free of
a rapist's seed, anyone
who knows how long the
drive through those green
croplands can last, anyone who's
learned how the glaciers slid
over those states like god's
hand wiping the earth
clean, would not be surprised
in the white machine's
cradled fist to see water rising,
not around your heart but
inside of it, would recognize
that dark crescent, your heart
a starfish washed to sand.
You should have known
this would happen, you
should have stayed under-
ground, you should have eaten
less salt, when the tears
poured down the sea-
kissed rocks, you should not
have swallowed them.

Pruning the Yew

It's been too long. You
fix the clippers

onto stem, limb,
trunk, gnaw the old

wood clean. There's
more to be cut all

around the yard, trees
you never planted, deadly

berries of Solomon's
seal, and the neighbor's

lilies creeping past the
fence: work enough for

a summer of days. But
this is the work you are

doing today, steel against
skin, listening to news

of the war as the yew
takes form in the ripe

thicket, sharpening all
the way to the heart

where a branch the size
of a child's leg hangs

almost free, ribbon
of white against moss-

dark trunk, somehow still
drawing life through

that ragged ligament,
still making leaves, still

the color of the
new grass, the lilies,

the poison fruit. There
is more to do for

this world than to
weep for it. But this

is the work you are
doing today.

iv.

In Answer to Your Question

Yes, I have tried yoga.
I have tried going gluten-free.
I have exercised every day
until my abs rippled
like an armadillo's shell.

And still my friend calls me up to say
that Pilates makes her feel ten years younger.

Yes, I have tried not eating
sugar. I read labels
like poetry, ruling out
fructose, nectars,
crystals, that confectionary
of risk. I turned away

each forbidden fruit, crunched
through bowls of cabbage
for breakfast until even
a raw banana slice
lay a faint music on my tongue.

And still my coworker stops me in the hallway
to tell me that sex has cured her migraines.

Yes, I have tried yoga, have pretzeled
my legs into shapes they
already knew, balanced, breathed, lain
down and shuddered my way
back up. I have stood, a crane

reaching to the sky in
tai chi class, I have gone back
to ward off monkeys, I have held the
ball of my own faltering, hand-
heavy persistence.

And still my family sends me articles
about the power of positive thinking.

Yes, I have
tried that too.

And still I will wake up
tomorrow
in the body I was given,

not trying to be crane, not
pretending I am winged,

just making my way
down the long hallways of
my body's house, stretching

my hands into tiger's
mouths, rounding my arms

to hold the answers you
never wanted to hear.

Elegy for A Mask Mandate

For a year, maybe two, I knew
that you loved me. I saw it
in your eyes, *the windows*

to the soul, the only part
of your face I needed to
see to believe. For a season,

maybe two, you went
with me everywhere, holding
hope like a parasol over

our heads. I thought we'd
created a new world, where
the sick and the well

could be citizens of
the same country. I held
your disinfected hand at

the theater, in the grocery
store, places I hadn't
gone for years. I knew there

would always be the
resisters, the ones who since
childhood called me *queer,*

cripple, lazy, hysterical. But
you muffled them with your
hand-sewn cotton, your

filter inserts, your N95s. We
learned to speak a new
vocabulary, to understand

what it means to protect
each other so we all survive. In
my home now, in my lonely

bed, I'm still speaking those
words to the silent house: *My mask
protects you. Your mask protects me.*

To the Doctor Who Said I Am Not One of The

people who don't even
look at their feet, who
shuffle the dust-

darkness, uncaring,
unlistening, un-
understanding their

skin's own
speech; to the
doctor who told

me not to worry
my heel's numbness
could rift to

crevasse, who
explained I was not
one of the kind

who forgets how
to remember to
heal; to that doctor

who clasped
my naked, fractured
foot, tracing its

trails and minnow-
skin, I say
I am she: I am

he: I am they
who surface the
darkness between

your words. Claw
and fibula, hoof and
toe; bunkmates,

burrow twins, rage-
siblings and sorrow-kin,
un-caring a way

together through
the 28 bones to find
our way home.

ACKNOWLEDGEMENTS

I'd like to thank the readers, listeners, and dear friends who have encouraged me over the last decade of rediscovering how to write poetry: my colleagues in the Departments of English and Gender and Women's Studies at the University of Wisconsin-Madison; Rita Mae Reese and the generous organizers and co-readers at the Arts and Literature Laboratory in Madison, WI; the hosts of Central Time on Wisconsin Public Radio; Jesse Lee Kercheval, Judy Mitchell, Oliver Baez Bendorf, Michael Snediker, Leah Lakshmi Piepzna-Samarasinha, Alison Kafer, Timothy Yu, Jim Ferris, Jesse Waggoner, Red Berry, Anoosh Jorjorian, Sarah McKibben, Joy Goldsmith, my dear brother Jordan Samuels, and all my beloved NADs.

I also owe many thanks to the talented poets who have been my teachers over the years: Bruce Beasley and Wendy Hesford at Oberlin; Ken McClane and the late A. R. Ammons at Cornell; and my beloved Barbara Helfgott Hyett.

Thank you to the Wisconsin Fellowship of Poets for awarding this collection with their first annual Chapbook Prize.

Finally, all my love to my son Charlie and my partner Jonathan who greet me with endless patience and exasperated love. I could do nothing without you.

These pieces, sometimes in earlier versions, appeared in the following:

Copper Nickel: "After The Procedure"
Colorado Review: "Yesterday I Apologized"
Tupelo Quarterly Online: "To the Doctor Who Said I Am Not One of The"
Massachusetts Review: "Elegy for A Mask Mandate." Reprinted in *Disability Intimacy*, ed. Alice Wong.
Rogue Agent: "On the Hospital"
ALL Review: "Plum Tomato"
Sow's Ear Quarterly: "Eggplant/Aubergine"
Brevity: "Sick and Well Time"
Mid-American Review: "Cigarette-Paper Scars"

NOTES

"Plum Tomato"
The first stanza references the poem "Ars Poetica" by Archibald MacLeish.

"My Mother Always Had Numbers."
"A woman/dying in her forties" references the poem "A Woman Dead in Her Forties" by Adrienne Rich.

"To the Doctor Who Said I Am Not One of The."
The title references the poem "I Am Not One of The" by Cheryl Marie Wade. The lines "I am she: I am he" are drawn from the poem "Diving into the Wreck" by Adrienne Rich.

ELLEN SAMUELS

ABOUT THE AUTHOR

Ellen Samuels is the author of a poetry collection *Hypermobilities* (Operating System, 2021) and a chapbook, *December Morning* (Finishing Line Press, 2002), as well as many works in disability studies. Her poetry and creative nonfiction have appeared in *Colorado Review, Copper Nickel, Nimrod, Brevity, Massachusetts Review, the Journal of the American Medical Association,* and many other venues. Her awards include two Lambda Literary Awards, two Pushcart nominations, and the FineLines Prize from *Mid-American Review.* She is an Emeritus Professor at the University of Wisconsin-Madison and is working on a book titled *Sick Time: What Chronic Life Tells Us.* She lives in Monona, WI with her partner and dog.

C&R PRESS CHAPBOOKS

C&R Press hosts two chapbook selection periods from June to September and November to March each year. The Summer Tide Pool and Winter Soup Bowl Chapbook Series are open to new and established writers in poetry, fiction, essay and other creative writing genres.

2024 WINTER SOUP BOWL
Your Body Should Be a Part of the World by Ellen Samuels

2023 SUMMER TIDE POOL
The Consolation of Geometry by Alice Campbell Romano

2023 WINTER SOUP BOWL
Dinner at Las Heras Allison A. deFreese's translation from the Spanish of Luciana Jazmín-Coronado

2022 SUMMER TIDE POOL
The Ice Beneath the Earth by Brian Ascalon Roley

2022 WINTER SOUP BOWL
tommy noun by Maurya Kerr

2021 SUMMER TIDE POOL
Rocketflower by Matthew Meade

2021 WINTER SOUP BOWL
We Face the Tremenedous Meat on the Teppan by Naoko Fujimoto

2020 WINTER SOUP BOWL
My Roberto Clemente by Rick Hilles

2019 SUMMER TIDE POOL
Inside the Orb of an Oracle by Dannie Ruth

2019 WINTER SOUP BOWL
The Magical Negro Reveals His Secret by Gabriel Green

2018 SUMMER TIDE POOL
Yell by Sarah Sousa

2018 WINTER SOUP BOWL
Paleotemptestology by Bertha Crombet

White Boys from Hell by Jeffrey Skinner

2017 SUMMER TIDE POOL
Atypical Cells of Undetermined Significance by Brenna Womer

2017 WINTER SOUP BOWL
Heredity and Other Inventions by Sharona Muir

On Inaccuracy by Joe Manning

2016 SUMMER TIDE POOL
Cuntstruck by Kate Northrop

Relief Map by Erin M. Bertram

Love Undefined by Jonathan Katz

2016 WINTER SOUP BOWL
Notes from the Negro Side of the Moon by Earl Braggs

A Hunger Called Music: A Verse History in Black Music
   by Meredith Nnoka